B♭ Trumpet

Audio Access
Included

Great Carols

Instrumental Solos for Christmas

Selected by James Curnow

Contents

PLAYBACK+
Speed • Pitch • Balance • Loop

To access audio, visit:
www.halleonard.com/mylibrary

Enter Code
1478-9291-5343-1277

ISBN 978-90-431-1886-6

CURNOW® MUSIC

EXCLUSIVELY DISTRIBUTED BY
HAL•LEONARD®

Visit Hal Leonard Online at
www.halleonard.com

Contact us:
Hal Leonard
7777 West Bluemound Road
Milwaukee, WI 53213
Email: info@halleonard.com

In Europe, contact:
Hal Leonard Europe Limited
42 Wigmore Street
Marylebone, London, W1U 2RN
Email: info@halleonardeurope.com

In Australia, contact:
Hal Leonard Australia Pty. Ltd.
4 Lentara Court
Cheltenham, Victoria, 3192 Australia
Email: info@halleonard.com.au

Great Carols

INTRODUCTION

This collection of some of the world's greatest Christmas carols was created for, and is dedicated to, Philip Smith, Principal Trumpet, New York Philharmonic Orchestra. The goal of these arrangements is to allow instrumentalists the opportunity to give praise and adoration to God through their musical abilities.

Though these arrangements were written specifically with Phil in mind, attention has been given to the needs of all of the individual instruments. Through the use of cued notes, players of differing ability levels will be able to perform these arrangements.

Each solo book includes online audio with a sample performance of each solo, as well as the accompaniment only. This will allow the performer to practice with the accompaniment when an accompanist is not available. The accompaniment track can also be used for performances if desired. Appropriate tuning notes have been added to the online audio to allow the soloist the opportunity to adjust their intonation to the intonation of the audio accompaniment. A separate piano accompaniment book is available.

May you enjoy using this collection and find it useful in extending your musical ministry.

Kindest regards,

James Curnow
President
Curnow Music Press, Inc.

Great Carols
B♭ Trumpet

Arranged by:
Stephen Bulla
Douglas Court
James Curnow
William Himes
Timothy Johnson
Kevin Norbury

Order number: HL44004680
ISBN 978-90-431-1886-6
Performed by Becky Shaw - Piano, Michael Rintamaa - Organ, Phil Smith - Trumpet
Recorded at Central Christian Church, Lexington , KY USA

Great Carols

PHILIP SMITH
Principal Trumpet
NEW YORK PHILHARMONIC

Philip Smith joined the New York Philharmonic as Co-Principal Trumpet in October 1978, and assumed the position of Solo Principal Trumpet in June 1988. His early training was provided at The Salvation Army, and continued under the training of his father, Derek Smith. He is a graduate of The Juilliard School, having studied with Edward Treutel and William Vacchiano, former Principal Trumpet of the New York Philharmonic. In January of 1975, while still at Juilliard, Mr. Smith was appointed to the Chicago Symphony Orchestra by Sir Georg Solti.

Mr. Smith has appeared regularly as soloist, recitalist, chamber orchestra performer and clinician. He has been featured as a soloist with the Philharmonic in over 75 performances under such conductors as Zubin Mehta, Kurt Masur, Erich Leinsdorf, Leonard Bernstein, Neeme Jarvi and Bram Tovey. Highlights have included the World Premiere of Joseph Turrin's Concerto with the New York Philharmonic, its subsequent European Premiere with the Leipzig Gewandhaus Orchestra, the U.S. Premiere of Jacques Hetu's Concerto, the World Premiere (2000) of Lowell Liebermann's Concerto, and the World Premiere (2003) of Siegfried Matthus' Double Concerto for Trumpet, Trombone and Orchestra. He has been a guest soloist with the Edmonton Symphony, Newfoundland Symphony, Columbus (Indiana) Symphony, Pensacola (Florida) Symphony, Hartford (Connecticut) Symphony, and Beaumont (Texas) Symphony.

Mr. Smith has also appeared with many symphonic wind ensembles including the United States "President's Own" Marine Band, La Philharmonic Des Vents Des Quebec, the Hanover Wind Symphony, the Ridgewood Concert Band, and many major university wind ensembles. He appeared at The College Band Directors National

Great Carols

Association Convention in Austin, Texas for the World Premiere (1999) of Turrin's "Chronicles" with the University of New Mexico Wind Ensemble.

An avid brass band enthusiast, Mr. Smith has been guest soloist with the United States Army Brass Band, Goteborg Brass (Sweden), Black Dyke Mills and Ridged Containers Bands (Britain), Hannaford Street Silver Band and Intrada Brass (Canada), and numerous American and Salvation Army Brass Bands. He appeared as featured soloist at the 1996 British Open Brass Band Championships in Manchester, England.

Mr. Smith is on the faculty at The Juilliard School and has appeared as recitalist and clinician at the Caramoor International Music Festival, Grand Teton Music Festival, Swiss Brass Week, Breman (Germany) Trumpet Days, Oslo (Norway) Trumpet Week, Harmony Ridge (Vermont) Festival, Scotia Festival of Music and numerous International Trumpet Guild conferences.

Mr. Smith has performed and recorded with the Canadian Brass, the Empire Brass, Chamber Music Society of Lincoln Center, Mostly Mozart Orchestra, Bargemusic and NY Virtuosi Chamber Symphony. His solo recordings include "Contest Solos" produced by the International Trumpet Guild, "Fandango" featuring New York Philharmonic Principal Trombonist Joseph Alessi and the University of New Mexico Wind Symphony (Summit), "My Song of Songs" with the New York Staff Band of the Salvation Army (Triumphonic), Copland's "Quiet City" (Deutsche Grammophone), New York Legends (CALA), Orchestral Excerpts for Trumpet (Summit), Ellen Taaffe Zwilich's Concerto for Trumpet and Five Instruments (New World), Bach's Brandenburg Concerto No. 2 (Koch), Walton's Façade (Arabesque), and The Trump Shall Resound and Repeat the Sounding Joy (Heritage/Resounding Praise).

Mr. Smith has recently been involved in a series of projects with Curnow Music Press, publishing music arrangements with demonstration CD's. These include "Great Hymns" for Trumpet, Piano and Organ, "Concert Studies" for Trumpet, and "Great Carols" for Trumpet, Piano and Organ. He has also been featured in a similar project entitled "Total Trumpet" featuring trumpet studies written by Michael Davis and demonstrated by Randy Brecker, Jim Hynes and Philip Smith, published by Hip-Bone Music.

Mr. Smith and his wife perform with their Gospel group, Resounding Praise, throughout North America. They have two adult children and live in New Jersey.

1. JOY TO THE WORLD

Arr. **James Curnow** (ASCAP)

2. GOOD CHRISTIAN MEN, REJOICE

Arr. **Douglas Court** (ASCAP)

66
mp
74
cresc.
f
82
mp
94
mf
cresc.
f
102
mf
f
To Piccolo Trumpet (Opt.)
114
122
mf
130
138

3. WHAT CHILD IS THIS?

Arr. **Stephen Bulla** (ASCAP)

Copyright © 2003 by **Curnow Music Press, Inc.**

4. O COME, ALL YE FAITHFUL

Based on an arrangement by Arlene Johnson

Arr. **Timothy Johnson** (ASCAP)

5. DING DONG MERRILY ON HIGH

Arr. **Kevin Norbury** (ASCAP)

6. IT CAME UPON THE MIDNIGHT CLEAR

Arr. **William Himes** (ASCAP)

7. ANGELS WE HAVE HEARD ON HIGH

Arr. **Stephen Bulla** (ASCAP)

8. O COME, O COME EMMANUEL

Arr. **Timothy Johnson** (ASCAP)

9. O LITTLE TOWN OF BETHLEHEM

Arr. **Douglas Court** (ASCAP)

Bb Trumpet

10. HE IS BORN

Arr. **James Curnow** (ASCAP)